‘Reading this book I stop
the air with joy. It is wa
It views older people as
planned by God in advance. Professor John Wyatt looks at the three major stages of our lives, from retirement to independent living, then dependency on others, and finally from living to dying. Each stage is imbued with God-given purpose: you experience “your heart’s deepest gladness” when you find yourself doing what you were created for. Older people have much to offer others, and the time to do it. Time to listen, to share the gospel, and to share insight and wisdom. John is now seventy and grateful for the wisdom he has gained over the years. He wouldn’t want to be twenty-five again, though it would be good to have a twenty-five year old body that didn’t ache so much. Finally, there is the finishing line and the falling asleep that Christ described with Lazarus. Death has been defeated by Christ on the cross, and we can look beyond the physical to the hidden glory.’

Louise Morse, writer and speaker,
Pilgrims’ Friend Society; author, *What’s Age Got To Do With It?*

'As someone who has recently moved from work to retirement, I found this book both encouraging and challenging. John Wyatt takes us through three significant transitions with huge personal implications for all of us. With sensitive pastoral insight and a fine grasp of biblical teaching he has given us a unique and immensely helpful book.'

Paul Mallard, author, *The Grace of Gratitude* and *Invest Your Suffering*

'In The Final Lap, *John provides a unique, comforting, and profound insight into the three major transitions that are likely to happen in the later stages of life, a topic that has been long waited for, for commentary and discussion. He gently confronts the fears our society often hold around life, post retirement, moving from independent living to dependence on others, and finally the transition from living to dying. This extremely digestible and positive read will encourage and inspire all who find themselves in later life, as well as those of us who offer pastoral care and support to this precious generation.'*

Pippa Cramer, MBE, Pastoral Care and Seniors Minister, Holy Trinity Church, Claygate

THE FINAL LAP

THE FINAL LAP

NAVIGATING THE TRANSITIONS OF LATER LIFE

JOHN WYATT

10 Publishing
a division of 10 of those.com

British Library Cataloguing in Publication Data
A record for this book is available from the British Library

ISBN: 978-1-915705-80-8

Designed by Pete Barnsley (CreativeHoot.com)

Printed in Denmark

10Publishing, a division of 10ofthose.com
Unit C, Tomlinson Road, Leyland, PR25 2DY, England

Email: info@10ofthose.com
Website: www.10ofthose.com

1 3 5 7 10 8 6 4 2

CONTENTS

INTRODUCTION:

THE MARATHON

'Life's a marathon not a sprint' – how often have you heard that familiar phrase? But as I reflect back on my life, having just celebrated my 70th birthday, the idea that life is like a long-distance race makes a lot more sense to me now than it used to. Certainly I'm in the 20-something mile of my own marathon, and those final laps are coming into view.

I've never actually run a marathon (10K was the best I could do), but I have some idea of what it must be like. Any long-distance run has different stages – the initial enthusiasm, the grinding uphill sections, the boring bits, that glorious downhill stretch when you feel as though you could run for ever. And every marathon runner needs to plan ahead for the final stages of the race. How are they going to survive if and when they 'hit the wall'? Experienced runners have told me that the final mile or so can be one of the most difficult and perilous parts of a marathon. And so runners plan ahead. They have their strategy to keep going through those last challenging phases of the race; conserving energy, keeping fluid intake up, having a snack ready for a final calorie boost.

The author of the book of Hebrews wrote, 'since we are surrounded by such a great cloud of witnesses, let us throw off everything that hinders and the sin that so easily entangles. And let us run with perseverance the race marked out for us, fixing our eyes on Jesus, the pioneer and perfecter of faith. For the joy that was set before him he endured the cross, scorning its shame, and sat down at the right hand of the throne of God' (Heb. 12:1-2).

We need to persevere if we are going to finish life well. Like long-distance runners, we need to prepare for the stages that still lie ahead. That's what this short book is all about. How can I prepare now for the final stages of the race? What are the challenges and opportunities that will come as I see the finish line drawing nearer?

Many of us have already run dark and dangerous sections in our race. We've already been through the valley David describes in Psalm 23, and we know that the race ahead of us will probably throw even more challenges our way. But each one of us has an individual course marked out for us. We don't choose our own path, we are given it. What's more, we're not alone. It's a group race. We are all in this together and we are here to encourage one another, to strengthen one another, to support and even carry one another along when we need to.

There's a great crowd of unseen witnesses all around us, watching us and cheering us on. How many millions of faithful Christian believers have run this race before us? We are not alone. But as the competitors enter the stadium for the final lap they are not taking a break and waving at the crowds. Their eyes are fixed on the course that's marked out for them. Hebrews tells us that we also need to fix our eyes on the one who has already completed the course: Jesus, the 'pioneer and perfecter' of the entire race. He was the one who both created the course, and the one who then ran it from beginning to end, showing us the way.

So if you, like me, have already been running for many miles, if you're hitting the wall or if the final lap and the finishing line are starting to loom, then this book is for you. We are going to be looking at three major transitions that are likely to happen in the later stages of the race. First, the transition from paid employment to what is laughingly called 'retirement', second the transition from independent living to dependence on others for our care needs, and finally the transition from living to dying, as we approach the finishing line itself.

1

HITTING THE WALL:

MOVING FROM WORK TO RETIREMENT

Germany was the first country to adopt a national pension programme in 1889, under the inspiration of Chancellor Otto von Bismarck. Initially Germany chose 70 years as the age at which a pension began, but this was later changed to 65 years as it became apparent that the state could afford this earlier age. Out of interest I looked up the average life expectancy in Germany in 1889. It was 40.3 years! The proportion of the population who actually survived to 65 and beyond must have been pretty small, and so there was no problem for the state to take on the economic cost of providing pensions.

But the world has changed. According to the UK Office of National Statistics (ONS), males who were aged 65 in 2020 can expect to live for an average of another 19.7 years, and for females it is 22 years. And according to the ONS, in 2045 the expected length of life beyond 65 is going to rise to 21.9 years for men and 24.1 for women. And that's just the average. There are going to be many people who will live into their 90s and beyond. Astonishingly, of babies who are born in 2022 in the UK, one in five girls, and one in six boys are expected to live beyond 100.[1]

Of course, these predictions may prove inaccurate, but they do give us a picture of how life expectancy is increasing. It's important to stop and think about what an extraordinary period we are living through. It's a new idea that in your late 50s or early 60s you can come to the end of your period of paid employment, and yet have another 30 years of healthy life ahead of you. Of course, many won't have the luxury of early retirement, but most will enjoy a number of years when they no longer have to work. It's never happened before; we are among the first to face this reality. And it raises huge questions.

Perhaps the most important question it raises for me is, 'What are old people for?' After all, there's an awful lot of us! And as followers of Christ, a related question is 'What are old people for in the Christian church family?'

To many health and economic planners, these improvements in life expectancy are threatening and disturbing. People talk about the 'demographic time bomb'. In Europe as a whole, one in thirteen of the population were over 65 in 1950. By 2035, it is thought that the ratio will be one in four.[2] The number of working 'economically productive' people is continuing to dwindle, whilst there is an ever-growing army of elderly people who are going on living for many decades, burning up health and social care resources, and their children's inheritances, instead of doing the decent thing and quietly 'popping their clogs'!

But this is a terribly depressing and negative way of looking at things. As Christians we know that all aspects of our lives are in God's hands, including their length. As much as the Apostle Paul wanted to be in the presence of his Lord in heaven, he was able to write, 'to live is Christ … If I am to go on living in the body, this will mean fruitful labour for me' (Phil. 1:21-22). His desire was to glorify God in this life for as many days as he was given. We should do the same! In his helpful and encouraging book *Finishing Well,* author Ian Knox has these inspiring words: 'A long life is a gift, not a curse. It is full of possibilities. And the gift is the gift of time.'[3]

PURPOSE IN LIFE

Now that the children have left home, my wife Celia and I have started taking breaks outside the school holidays. We have come across a lot of older couples who seem to be having a great time burning up the children's inheritance! Exotic foreign holidays, restaurant meals, hobbies, cruises. Ticking off items on their bucket list.

If you look at secular ideas of retirement, they largely seem to be, 'You've worked extremely hard for most of your life. And now it's time to enjoy yourself. You owe it to yourself. Do the things you've always wanted to do. Now's your opportunity.' In other words, once you have retired you can live the rest of your life in contented selfishness.

But in reality, do you want to spend the next 20 or 30 years in contented selfishness? The truth is that we all desire meaning in life, not just recreation, however lovely that can be for a time. We all need something to get up for in the morning. In

Philippians 1, Paul desired to go on living so he could love and serve the church. We need direction, goals, purpose. But as our paid work comes to an end and our energies decrease, it can be hard to know where to find the meaning in life we each require.

For many of us, throughout our adult lives, identity and meaning have come, at least in part, from our employment. The first question we are asked when we meet a stranger is 'What do you do?' The prospect of stopping work is absolutely terrifying. This is particularly the case for people who have the privilege of carrying out fulfilling jobs. I happen to know that it's very common among doctors, because so many doctors find their employment fulfilling, stretching and rewarding. It's a job which gives social status, meaning and purpose, not to mention a nice secure income. And then suddenly I find that I have been compulsorily retired, I have lost my medical licence to practise, and I am on the medical scrap heap. And of course it's not just doctors who feel that their purpose and significance is focussed on their work. If we are honest, most of us have to admit that our work plays a large part in our identity. So what am I going to do now that empty weeks and months are opening up before me? Am I really going to spend the rest of my life on the golf course or watching TV?

THE WALL?

Marathon runners talk about the experience of hitting the wall – a sudden and overwhelming fatigue around the 20-mile mark of the race. Motivation plummets and negative thoughts flood in. Retiring might feel a bit like that for some. Certainly my own experience of retiring from medical practice as a consultant paediatrician in the NHS was surprisingly disorientating and hard. I was looking forward to retirement, I was counting the days. But when it actually happened it was strange and difficult. When I was working as a consultant on the neonatal intensive care unit, whenever I walked onto the unit there were things that needed doing. 'We need to make a decision about Baby X. When can you talk to the parents of Baby Y? We need to start the ward round! There's a new baby we are worried about. There's a group of medical students who have turned up, what do you want to do with them?' Everybody is wanting a piece of me. And my first reaction is to say, 'I can't cope. Please get off my back. Give me a bit of space…' But of course, all these demands are sending you the message that you're an important member of the team, you've actually got something to contribute.

A few months after I finally stopped working in the NHS, I returned to the hospital for some reason. I walked onto the neonatal unit and a nurse, whom I didn't know, came up to me with a polite and professional smile, 'Hello, can I help you?' And I thought to myself, 'Yes, I'm yesterday's news. I'm surplus to requirements. I don't have anything to contribute here anymore.' That's the painful reality which many of us face when we come to the end of our careers.

If we place our entire identity, our meaning and our purpose in our employment, then retirement will be a devastating blow. We hit the wall and there's nothing to keep us going. Certainly I went through an unsettled period of questioning, seeking and exploring possibilities interspersed with periods of deep internal uncertainty.

Just like runners aim to avoid a painful wall experience by good preparation, Helen Calder in her helpful course *Retiring Well* advises people to start thinking and planning for their future one to two years *before* retirement. Looking back, I can certainly see the wisdom of this. I might have avoided some of that period of unsettled, painful questioning if I had started planning for retirement in advance.

LOOK FOR THE ACTIVITIES WHICH ENERGISE

As we make the transition from paid employment to retirement, we have to recognise that we all have *shoulds* and *oughts* and *musts*. We all have duties and responsibilities to others that we cannot and should not avoid. But the problem with the *shoulds* and the *oughts* is that these responsibilities and duties tend to sap our energy. They drain us. And as we all know, as we get older we are starting to run out of energy. Our reserves are not what they used to be. And so if we spend too much of our time on the *shoulds* and the *oughts* we may find that we're running on empty. This is the opposite problem to contented selfishness – being overly duty-driven.

So instead, we need to be looking for those areas of service where you say to yourself, 'I would just love to…'; 'Wouldn't it be wonderful if…'; 'Wouldn't that be amazing if...' Because these are the areas, the concerns, the activities, the needs that energise and motivate us. These are the things that thrill our heart, and that give meaning and purpose to our lives.

A single missionary whom I shall call Ruth, was a wonderful example to me of joy, enthusiasm and fruitfulness in her retirement years. She even managed to complete a research thesis and obtain a higher degree in her 80s. But her greatest love was meeting new people and listening to and encouraging others. In the final years of her life she took to travelling the London Underground from one end to the other, simply praying silently and looking for opportunities for conversation with strangers. 'I think of myself as a kind of movable tabernacle,' she explained to me once, as she talked about how the Holy Spirit directed and worked through her to touch the lives of those she met.

Ruth found joyful purpose in reaching out to those around her in a way which suited her God-given gifts and personality. Author Frederick Buechner writes, 'The kind of work God usually calls you to is the kind of work that *(a)* you need most to do and *(b)* that the world most needs to have done.' He summarises his thought in this beautiful word, 'The place God calls you to is the place where your deep gladness and the world's deep hunger meet.'[4]

As a scientist I can't help seeing this as a graph. On one axis is, 'The way you're made'; your heart's deepest gladness. And along the other axis is, 'What the world really needs.' And where these two lines meet, that is your Christian vocation, that is what you were created for – the unique place where your heart's deepest gladness meets the world's deepest needs.

Now I recognise that this is a somewhat idealistic perspective. It isn't always like that. There are times when our service – our doing what is right – is not so much about joy now as about grit and determination and struggle. And yet, it seems to me there's something very profound in this thought, particularly for older people. As we confront the transition from paid employment to the next phase of our lives, we need to find new energy and new purpose. And that energy lies where we can serve others in a way we are passionate about.

I think it's valuable to reflect back on our own lives to this point. When were those moments when my heart sang? When were those moments when I said, 'This is what I was made for; this is my deepest joy'? The truth is that these moments don't happen very often. But when they do happen they are a kind of epiphany or revelation of the way that God has made me, of my own unique wiring, and the things which set me alight.

I know it sounds strange, but I can remember extraordinary moments on the neonatal intensive care unit when I was caring for a baby that was dying, and I was trying to support the parents. There were tears, sadness and intense grief. But somewhere deep inside, there was also a deep conviction, 'Yes, this is what I was made for. This is why I was put here.' Or at other moments in my life, when I have been trying to explain a complex spiritual idea to another person and watched their eyes light up as they said, 'Oh, yes, now I get it. Yes!' Or just over the last weeks, when playing with our granddaughter, 'Yes, this, this is what I was made for.' These are rare moments of epiphany, of revelation. They are telling us something deep about the unique way that we are wired and the reason we have been placed here on the earth. And so these rare moments can give us pointers to how we can love and serve others, finding our heart's deepest gladness for this next phase of our life.

These motivations often change as we go through our life. Certainly many of my deepest longings have changed for me now I am in my 70s compared with when I was in my 20s and 30s. But at each stage of the race, God is saying to us, look for joy in serving Jesus. It's joy that will keep you going. Of course, the biblical understanding of joy is not the same as a kind of superficial happiness. It's a wellspring, a rich gladness that comes from knowing that you are serving God and that you are becoming the person that he made you to be.

In Psalm 103 David talks of the God 'who satisfies your desires with good things so that your youth is renewed like the eagle's' (Ps. 103:5). In the literal Hebrew the text says God satisfies us with 'the good' so that our youth is renewed. As our desires are satisfied, our energy is renewed. And we become like the eagle, who merely holds out its wings and is driven aloft by the thermals. This is a beautiful metaphor for the Holy Spirit lifting us effortlessly by his power, energising us and leading us onwards.

We should never forget that running the race is ultimately all about joy. There's joy in the running and joy to come at the end of the race. Returning to the book of Hebrews, we see Jesus ran his race focused on joy: 'For the joy that was set before him he endured the cross, scorning its shame, and sat down at the right hand of the throne of God' (Heb. 12:2).

Jesus endured the race which led all the way to the cross for the joy that was marked out for him along the way and at the end. There were clearly deep moments of joy for Jesus as he spent time with his closest friends, as he saw lives transformed, as he spent time with children, 'sinners' and the nobodies of society. And he was motivated and energised to go through the unimaginable agony of Gethsemane, bearing the sins of the entire world, for joy. As he was crucified he was thinking about the resurrection, he was anticipating all that was going to happen. The joy of meeting Mary Magdalene in the garden, of seeing his disciples again in the upper room and of the barbecue on the beach. He set his thoughts on the future wedding feast of the Lamb. It was joy that kept him running the race. It's all about joy.

WHAT ARE OLD PEOPLE FOR?

As we make the transition from paid employment to retirement, it seems to me that the question 'What are old people for?' takes on new relevance. In the remainder of this chapter, I'll explore a number of ways in which older people are able to make a special contribution to those around them.

Availability

When we are in the midst of our working lives, making space and time for people can seem almost impossible. I remember occasions when my wife and I had to plan months ahead just to find time to meet up with friends or invite someone for a meal. But now that I am no longer in full-time employment, it has become much easier to make myself available to others at short notice. And in our busy, pressurised and demanding world, when so many working people are barely hanging on by their fingertips, having older people around who are prepared to make themselves available becomes a vital ministry. It's a gift that we can offer to others. We don't have to have specialised skills in counselling or pastoral care. We just need to be able to be there, to offer a listening ear and an encouraging word.

Life wisdom

It's often been said that 'We live life forwards but we understand it backwards.' And I for one am grateful for the (albeit limited) wisdom and insights that I have gained over the last 70 years of my life. We live in a world which idolises youth and in which so many older people are trying to pretend that they are 25 again. But to be honest I really don't want to be 25 again! Of course, it would be good to have a body that didn't ache and get quite so tired, but I'm extremely grateful for what I have learnt since over the past 50 years. As older people we have the privilege of being able to offer some of the life wisdom we have gleaned along the way.

When we're young, it's easy to think we've got life sorted out. It's all a bit black and white. As long as you do this, follow this teaching, keep this diet, follow these rules, then everything is going to work out fine. Well, by the time you get to your 60s and beyond, most of us have come to the realisation that life is just not that simple. Sometimes people try genuinely to do their best and terrible things result. Bad things seem to happen to good people, and good things happen to bad people. Those you trusted and thought were dependable turned out not to be as good as you thought, and so on, and so on. As older people we can accept that life is not always clear cut. It's not that we don't believe there are such realities as good and evil, right and wrong. But we also know that real life can be messy and unpredictable. So we are called to listen to others in a gentle, non-judgemental way. And I think it can be particularly helpful to share from our own experiences the ways that God has blessed us in spite of our failures and weaknesses.

Intergenerational friendships

As a younger man I had the immense privilege of developing close friendships with a number of older people who chose to reach out to me, inviting me for meals, making themselves available, offering love, support, wisdom and prayers. Looking back I can see that these close friendships were deeply influential and transformative for the direction of my life and service, inspiring and moulding me into the person that I have become.

But deep and intimate intergenerational friendships seem to be becoming increasingly unusual in our society. It seems as though many older people have become very reluctant to reach out in friendship to younger people in their churches or communities. Some have lost their confidence when it comes to supporting younger members of their community. 'I'm not at all sure I've got anything to offer. I don't get half the things they talk about. I don't understand social media, dating apps, computer games. I don't understand the kind of lives they live.' It's easy to conclude that we have nothing to offer.

But that isn't true. Everyone reading these words has something to offer to a younger person, even if it's just a listening ear, showing that you care, telling them that you would like to understand their lives and pray for the issues they face. Young people need friends with life wisdom, people who are available, who will listen to them and love them and pray for them. So can I gently suggest perhaps you could take the initiative? Don't wait to be asked. All it takes is to offer a cup of coffee or a walk together.

Since retirement, God has given me a number of medical students, junior doctors and young scientists as friends. I am intentionally trying to invest in their lives by meeting up with them from time to time. It's very much a two-way process. I am learning as much from spending time with them as they are from me. And as our friendships deepen I have found that it is often most helpful to share a little from my own experiences of failure and struggle. By making myself more vulnerable and sharing some of my own challenges, I'm encouraging them to be more honest and open with me. Obviously, this takes wisdom and discernment to know how much to share and how to do it. Our first responsibility is to be listening and caring for the other person, not to focus on ourselves. But when it seems appropriate there is a place for opening up about our own experiences of the deep waters of suffering, failure or bereavement, as well as our faith and hope in Christ.

Sharing our faith

Many of us find that, now we are no longer restrained by professional and employment concerns, it is easier to be more open with others about our faith. Despite the rising life expectancy, older people are frequently confronted with their mortality and for some this has led to a greater openness to talking about deeper issues than in younger years – the meaning of life, the reality of guilt, the possibility of forgiveness and what happens beyond the grave. Ian Knox points out that despite attending church, many retired people do not have a deep personal faith in Christ. This presents us with an opportunity! Knox says, 'I am finding, time and again that many of these faithful churchgoers do want to make a real move in their lives, with a longing to come into a deep relationship with God through a personal trust in Jesus.'[5]

Prayerfulness

When I was working as a front-line doctor and research scientist, I often put in 80-90 hours a week. When it came to prayer, sometimes the best I could manage was to use the ten-minute walk from our house to the underground station. I used that brief time to pray and prepare for the coming shift in the hospital. But once retired, most of us now have more time and opportunity to learn more about praying for others.

In our family, we have some wonderful examples of praying grandparents. My father was a praying grandparent. He used to use the selection of Bible passages called *Daily Light,* which have readings for every day of the year. My father wrote into his well-used volume all the important anniversaries and events that had occurred on each particular day. He would use those notes to pray for his extended family and friends around the world.

My wife's mother has also been another wonderful role model of a praying grandparent. In her 80s she taught herself how to use email, so that she could keep in touch with her thirteen grandchildren. She asked them to all send her an email once a week giving her the details of what they were doing on each day of the coming week – so that she could pray for them individually every day. It became very important to each grandchild to know that Granny was praying for them. They wanted to make sure that Granny knew about the coming exam, the new friends they were making and the challenges they were facing, so that she would pray. Maybe you don't have biological grandchildren. There are spiritual children that you can contact to tell them that you are praying for them. As we enter into the later stages of life, even if we suffer from increasing physical limitations, prayerfulness for the younger generations is a calling that each one of us can fulfil.

No runner wants to hit the wall and spend the last six miles of the marathon dragging themselves along. But unlike running, hitting retirement doesn't have to mean a long-lasting slog for the remainder of the race. We can recover from the potentially unsettling change and go on to flourish, running our final miles with purpose and joy.

2

THE HOME STRAIGHT:

MOVING FROM INDEPENDENCE TO DEPENDENCE

After all the ups and downs of our race, the home straight brings a new challenge for many of us. In this chapter we are looking at this next stage in the marathon, the transition from independence to dependence. And, however uncomfortable it is to think about, most of us are going to go through a final phase when we become dependent on other people for some or all of our personal care needs. It would be crazy to run a marathon and not plan ahead for the final lap, desperately hoping we can avoid it. No experienced marathon runner would think in that way. They prepare ahead for the challenges of that crucial final stage, planning for how they're going to cope. We need to do the same.

In the second letter to the Corinthians, the Apostle Paul talks honestly about his struggles. He describes himself as hard pressed, perplexed and struck down. But through it all, he writes, 'we do not lose heart. Though outwardly we are wasting away, yet inwardly we are being renewed day by day. For our light and momentary troubles are achieving for us an eternal glory that far outweighs them all. So we fix our eyes not on what is seen, but on what is unseen, since what is seen is temporary, but what is unseen is eternal' (2 Cor. 4:16-18).

As we think about the home straight of the race, and the transition into dependence, sharing Paul's perspective is vital if we are going to run with perseverance. Paul distinguishes between 'what is seen' which is temporary, and 'what is unseen' which is eternal. So much of our modern culture is focussed on the surface appearance, and especially on the way that our faces and bodies look. This is particularly true of social media platforms where people can spend hours using software tools, changing and tweaking their appearance to meet socially acceptable standards. Many young people in particular seem to be dissatisfied with their bodies. But it's not only young people who worry about their appearance. For many of us as we age we worry about the wrinkles and the saggy skin and all the marks of ageing. We become fearful about our outward appearance.

We also live in a society which is obsessed with the idea of having absolute freedom to choose our own path. Philosophers call this 'the principle of autonomy', a word taken from the Greek *auto-nomos*, meaning self-rule, or more crudely, 'My rules, my way.' In medical ethics today, this principle guides all medical practice. Patients should be free to make their own rules. Of course, in reality, it doesn't quite work like that. No one is genuinely free to make up their own rules for living. It's a myth, but a very powerful one. For many of us, the ability to choose and make our own decisions is the most important thing in our lives. Therefore as we approach the end of our lives, the prospect of losing our ability to direct ourselves, to be robbed of 'autonomy', is seen as the greatest possible threat.

Many of those campaigning for the right to choose how and when they die are not young people, but those in their 70s and beyond. They are classic Baby Boomers who are used to living their lives with high levels of control. And as they face the possibility of losing that control through old age and illness, they are terrified about what might happen. It's this fear which drives them to say, 'We've got to change the law so that I can kill myself or be killed by a doctor. I'm not prepared to go through that terrible undignified stage of depending on other people, of losing my dignity.'

But what the Christian faith teaches us is something profoundly different. Instead of independence being the greatest good, we learn that dependence is all part of the design. It's the way that we have been made. God makes people in his own image. Human beings are God-like beings. Each one of us reflects the character of God himself. It's utterly astonishing; God chooses a small, fragile, carbon-based life form to carry his glorious image.

The first human being was created from the dust of the ground (Genesis 2:7). In Hebrew the word for human, *adam*, is derived from *adamah*, which is the Hebrew word for ground. So in the literal Hebrew, human beings are 'groundlings'. And the same thought is expressed in the English word 'human', which is taken from the word *humus*. Put aside all thoughts of Mediterranean food, this *humus* is what you find in the compost heap. And that's what we are made out of. God chose to create us out of the ground.

I've come to realise how profound this is. For Christians, it is not a design flaw that we become dependent on others. Human beings are *designed* to be dependent on others, to be limited and vulnerable. Even before the Fall, it was not good for Adam to be alone. He needed Eve. It was only together they could fulfil God's command to 'Be fruitful and increase in number; fill the earth and subdue it' (Gen. 1:28). Surely God could have chosen to create us differently. He could have chosen to make us wonderful, glorious, dynamic beings, with no need for others. Think of the heavenly seraphim described by Isaiah in his vision. They are crying 'Holy, holy, holy' and the entire Temple is shaking at the sound of their voices (Is. 6:1-4). God could have created us like those radiant and powerful beings. But instead, he chose to make us fragile and dependent.

Not only are we designed to depend on God, we're designed to depend on one another.

You and I came into the world locked into a network of relations that we did not choose, with a mother and father, grandparents, siblings, aunts and uncles, friends and carers. Without being consulted, we began life utterly reliant on them! And in Christian thinking this was not some bizarre fluke or accident, it was an essential part of what it means to be human.

THE NARRATIVE OF A HUMAN LIFE

We come into the world as helpless beings, totally dependent on another's love and care. We go through a phase of our lives when other people depend on us. We protect them, care for them, feed them, pay for them. And then most of us will end our physical lives totally dependent on the love and care of others. We will need other people to feed us, protect us and care for us. There is a strange symmetry in our human lives. And this is not a terrible, degrading inhuman reality. It's part of the design; it's part of the narrative of a human life. We're created to be bonded together in lives of mutual dependence. God places us in our biological families, and for those of us who are Christian believers, God also places us in a Christian church family, the local church community.

This was brought home to me in a poignant way after my mother had been tragically struck down with a rapidly progressive form of dementia. She could do nothing for herself and she became totally dependent on 24-hour nursing care. I was visiting her towards the end and someone put a yoghurt pot and teaspoon into my hand. I was trying to feed her. 'Open your mouth, here it comes…' And then the thought struck me that this was exactly what she used to do with me, all those years ago. I could remember her very words as she fed me. But now the tables were turned. And I remember thinking at the time, 'Perhaps this is the way it was meant to be.' I was learning more of what it meant to be a son, and she was learning more of what it meant to be a mother.

The Apostle Paul wrote in the letter to the Galatians, 'Carry each other's burdens, and in this way you will fulfil the law of Christ' (Gal. 6:2). Many people find it easier to face carrying someone else's burdens than allowing themselves to be carried, but God created every single one of us to need others.

Perhaps the next time you hear someone say, 'I just don't want to be a burden to anybody', you should gently respond, 'You are meant to be a burden to me, and I am meant to be a burden to you. And the life that God has given us is one of mutual burdensomeness!'[6]

Theologian Gilbert Meilaender wrote an article entitled, 'I Want to Burden My Loved Ones', in which he says, 'Is this not in large measure what it means to belong to a family: to burden each other – and to find almost miraculously, that others are willing, even happy, to carry such burdens.'[7] Of course, I know that not all families are like this. You may have a very painful and difficult family background, and you may have a very painful church family context, but it seems to me that as we face the challenges of an ageing population, and the difficulties of providing enough carers and proper social care, then the coming challenge to the Christian community will be 'Can we live in a way in which we genuinely carry one another's burdens?'

I know that genuine practical caring is tough. It's hard and it's challenging. We can't sentimentalise what practical caring involves. And I also know that many older people continue to worry about the possibility of them becoming dependent in the future. Many people, including some who have a strong Christian faith, have deep anxieties about what the future might hold, and what would happen if they were to become unable to care for themselves. They know that they should be prepared to accept becoming dependent on others, but they are painfully aware of the apparent inadequacies of the health and social care that is available.

So as we prepare for the transition from independence to dependence, I think we need to discuss these questions in advance with our loved ones, with our friends and with professionals who can advise us about the options. And those of us who have older relatives and friends can be asking these questions. 'Where would you like to be looked after in the future? What would be the best arrangement for your care? How can we plan ahead? What changes do we need to make to your accommodation now, so that you can cope as you become frailer?' Of course I understand that these conversations can be painful and embarrassing. But we need to discuss these issues openly with our loved-ones, now before the crisis strikes.

When we contemplate the likelihood that we ourselves will become dependent on others, it is easy to give way to fear. We need to remind ourselves again of the words of Ian Knox: 'A long life is a gift, not a curse. It is full of possibilities. And the gift is the gift of time.' And even dependence has its possibilities. It has possibilities of internal growth, of learning more about gratitude and joy. And for those of us who are Christian believers, dependence can lead to a new closeness to Christ.

THE INCARNATION

Not only did God choose to create us as limited, fragile and dependent beings, in Jesus he himself took on flesh. This is both amazing and wonderful – as well as being utterly unexpected. The living God himself, the God of total power and authority, chooses voluntarily to turn himself into a human baby in the person of Jesus. We are so familiar with the Christmas story that we have forgotten how utterly shocking it is.

When the first Christians started talking and preaching about the Incarnation and the Christmas miracle, the general reaction from the philosophers and thinkers of the day was 'That's just disgusting and vulgar.' It was simply inconceivable that the God of the universe would turn himself into a real baby who was swaddled, breastfed and washed by his mother. And yet, that is the scandal of the Christmas story. God chooses to make himself utterly and totally dependent. And at the end of his life on earth, the God of total power and authority is stretched out on a cross with nails through his hands. And through parched lips, he says, 'I am thirsty' (Jn. 19:28). He can do nothing for himself.

That's where we see God's power and glory revealed – in dependence, in vulnerability. God himself needed human arms to cuddle him, clothe him, clean him, keep him warm. He needed a human mother. In fact he entrusted his entire human existence to fallible human beings. And yet Christ's divine status and his dignity was in no way impaired or demeaned. Even in those moments of total dependence as a baby, or on the cross, he is still the second Person of the Trinity, he is still upholding the entire cosmos by the word of his power (Col. 1:17; Heb. 1:3).

So what we see in this is that to be dependent on others is not a degrading and dehumanising process. In fact when we experience this kind of dependence, we experience a tiny reflection of what the Son of God out of love chose for himself. He chose this route of making himself dependent, in order to reveal his glory as our Saviour. Glory in weakness.

As we face our final lap of the race, even if we end up being cared for by others, even if we need to be fed and washed and have our bottoms wiped, our dignity and status as a beloved child of God is not in the slightest altered or demeaned. I will still be the person known, loved and upheld by God himself.

SOMEONE WITH SKIN ON

Of course, we mustn't sentimentalise or romanticise the experience of dependence. The reality of depending on others for our care needs can feel distressing, painful and humiliating. Some years ago I developed a severe psychiatric illness and I ended up in a locked psychiatric ward. It was an intensely humiliating and painful experience. In my depression I became convinced that my whole life, my professional career and everything that I had worked for had been destroyed. It was a terrible experience, a kind of a personal hell. And if you had talked to me at that time about God, it meant nothing to me. 'God' was just a word with three letters. But the one thing that penetrated my darkness was the realisation that I was still loved by human beings. My wife came to the ward and gave me a wordless cuddle. And my spiritual father, John Stott, telephoned me in the locked ward. He said, 'I value your friendship, John.' And it brought tears to my eyes.

I learned from that painful time. However deep the pit, however locked people are in their own suffering, human love can penetrate. In fact, as we care for others we are called to represent God's invisible love in human form. I've often told the story of a little girl who's trying to get to sleep in her bedroom.[8] Her mother is downstairs and busy in the kitchen. And a little voice comes down the stairs. 'Mummy, mummy, I'm scared about the dark. Can you come and give me a cuddle?' And Mummy calls up 'No, I'm sorry darling, I'm too busy at the moment.' 'Can Daddy come and give me a cuddle?' 'No, Daddy's very busy too.' And then because Mummy is a very pious lady she adds, 'Just remember that God is with you. And he can give you a cuddle.' There is a pause and then the little voice comes down the stairs, 'But Mummy, I need someone with skin on…'

It's a profound story. Because we are physical beings, made out of flesh – *humus* – we need God's love to be revealed to us in physical form. We need physical arms around us. We need to hear a physical voice saying words of comfort. Those of us who are called to care for other people have the amazing privilege of showing God's love 'with skin on'. Those of us receiving this tangible care have the privilege of experiencing our Father's love through others.

For me there was a long and slow process of psychiatric and spiritual recovery and healing which continued over many years. And as I was recovering, I remembered some words attributed to the medieval writer Bernard of Clairvaux, 'Christ himself kisses us in the love of our friends.' I realised that Jesus himself was reaching out to me in that locked psychiatric ward. He was there in the love of my closest friends.

The healing and recovery process took many years. But with that slow recovery, I gradually came to realise that in my experience of dependence, God had given me a strange kind of gift. It was a gift I desperately didn't want to have, and had fought against. But God has given me this gift in order to try to help others who have their own mental health issues and struggles. I can empathise with others in despair because I have been through it myself. And I am learning what the Apostle Paul means when he refers to his 'thorn in the flesh' (2 Cor. 12:7): 'But [Jesus] said to me, "My grace is sufficient for you, for my power is made perfect in weakness." Therefore I will boast all the more gladly about my weaknesses, so that Christ's power may rest on me' (2 Cor. 12:9).

So as we approach a period when we become dependent on others, we need to see that despite the suffering and apparent humiliation, this can be part of God's calling on our lives. Doctor John Dunlop encourages Christians to remember that we are totally dependent on God for salvation and, in fact, all of the Christian life requires us to be willing to be served – by God and by others. He writes, 'At the end of life, it's good to be less self-sufficient, and trust God more fully.'[9]

As we are called to gradually and voluntarily give up our freedom to others, may we let go progressively, willingly and graciously. John Dunlop continues, 'Many of the losses associated with ageing are inevitable, and often forced upon us. But some things we can choose to give up voluntarily. When we can see the losses coming, I have observed that it's much better to recognise them, plan for them, and make changes gradually and proactively rather than waiting for a crisis to force a drastic change.'[10]

CONTENTMENT

I remember that John Stott struggled with the reality of dependence in his final year of life. He had a severe disabling illness, and his razor-sharp intellect and memory were declining. He was finding it harder to communicate. But this is what he said of his experience of disability, 'I would not say that I am happy, but I am learning to be content.' He was consciously echoing the words of the Apostle Paul. 'I have learned the secret of being content in any and every situation, whether well fed or hungry, whether living in plenty or in want. I can do all this through him who gives me strength' (Phil. 4:12-13). At the end of his life when Paul was imprisoned and facing execution he could write, 'godliness with contentment is great gain. For we brought nothing into the world, and we can take nothing out of it' (1 Tim. 6:6-7).

In the previous chapter, we asked the question, 'What are old people for?' And we looked at a list of opportunities we have when retired: increased availability for others, life wisdom, time to pray more and to share our faith. I find it very striking and reassuring that most of these opportunities can continue in some form even as we become dependent on others. We can still offer friendship, life wisdom, prayerfulness, and we can still share our faith and hope with others.

We can still provide positive models of letting go, we can be looking towards the future, we can be expressing gratitude and leave a legacy to those who come after. Dependence doesn't strip us of any of these opportunities. And so as the Apostle Paul reminds us, 'we do not lose heart. Though outwardly we are wasting away, yet inwardly we are being renewed day by day. For our light and momentary troubles are achieving for us an eternal glory that far outweighs them all. So we fix our eyes not on what is seen, but on what is unseen, since what is seen is temporary, but what is unseen is eternal' (2 Cor. 4:16-18).

3

THE FINISH LINE:

MOVING FROM LIFE TO DEATH

In the previous chapters we looked at the transitions from paid employment to retirement, and from independence to dependence. Now we turn to the third and final transition – from living to the process of dying. The race is almost won. We're on the final lap and the finishing line is in full view. As you read these words, I'm aware that many of us have watched a loved-one die. You may have watched someone who didn't die well. I'm conscious that my words may trigger memories that may be positive or extremely painful.

The Christian faith teaches us that death is an enemy (1 Cor. 15:26). And therefore we should never welcome or hasten death. That's the fundamental reason why, from a Christian perspective, assisted suicide and euthanasia are wrong. We should not welcome or introduce death into our lives. And yet, by God's grace, at the end of our lives that enemy death can be transformed miraculously into what C.S. Lewis called 'a severe mercy'[11]. It becomes a gateway to heaven.

As we face our own mortality, it's inevitable that we will be asking the questions, 'How am I going to die? Who will be there with me? What will I experience?' It's important that we talk and reflect together about these things, because dying has become a taboo subject in our society. It's been pushed out of our consciousness. Dying has been medicalised. It happens in hospitals, behind discreet curtains. But we need to talk and think about our own deaths before the crisis strikes.

Physician John Dunlop, who has had the experience of caring for many dying people wrote, 'One thing I have learned is that dying well is rarely a coincidence. Rather, it results from choices made throughout life. After all, dying well is nothing more than living well, right up to the end.'[12] I have had the privilege of accompanying many dying people over the years, witnessing the difference their faith brings.

Dying well doesn't usually happen by chance. It happens because we have been thinking and planning for it in advance. The experienced marathon runner has been thinking about, and planning for, crossing the finishing line for many miles. Runners say that approaching the finishing line can be a dangerous time. You may have survived for 26 miles but it can all go horribly wrong in those last few yards. Some runners collapse and never get up again, just within sight of the line.

We want to be those who run with perseverance right to the end, our eyes on Jesus and his welcome into eternity. The process of dying itself can lead to new opportunities and possibilities. In fact, our final days and weeks can turn into a strange kind of adventure. In this chapter I want to focus on some of the opportunities that dying well can bring.

SPIRITUAL GROWTH

Minister Rico Tice was visiting Ann Neller in hospital. She was an elderly single lady who had been a church member for many years. She was now close to death. As Rico entered the ward he gave her name and asked a nurse where she was. 'Oh you mean Gabby – we all call her the Angel Gabriel because she shines.'

One of the profound spiritual lessons that dying has to teach us is learning to see beyond the superficial appearance of our humanity to recognise the spiritual reality and beauty that lies beneath. In our materialistic and image-conscious culture, it is the outward appearance which tends to dominate our thoughts and preoccupations. When we see our own bodies, or those of the people we love most, deteriorating because of disease or ageing, becoming wrinkly, flabby, and distorted, we are secretly appalled. But we need spiritual eyes to see that there is more here than meets the eye – by God's grace there can be a hidden glory.

As we approach the finishing line, there is an opportunity for us to be growing and flourishing internally and spiritually, even as our bodies deteriorate. In the next section we'll look at several different ways in which internal growth and even spiritual beauty can be nurtured and encouraged in the last weeks and months of our lives.

HEALING, BUILDING, CELEBRATING AND COMPLETING RELATIONSHIPS

Dying well is an opportunity for healing from the inside. It's an opportunity for broken relationships to be healed and restored, even after many years of fracture and hostility. It's also an opportunity for good relationships to be made stronger, more open and more honest. It's an opportunity for sharing from the heart and saying sorry and thank you to those who are closest to us. In order to die well, I have to be at peace with God and at peace with the most important people in my life.

As a person approaches the finishing line, it sometimes seems as though they have a kind of 'relational authority'. The dying person is given an opportunity to say things, to encourage others, to mend broken relationships in a way which might have felt impossible before. Our words to our loved ones can be a special gift that will stay with them for the rest of their lives. One way we can leave a legacy is by writing letters, or recording an audio or video message. If you're a parent or a grandparent, here's an opportunity to write a letter or record a message for your loved-ones to encourage them, to remind them, to point to the faithfulness of God in your life. We can verbalise the kind of intimate and significant truths that we sometimes find so difficult to express in normal life.

To talk of 'completing relationships' may sound rather strange. There's a sense in which as we go on into eternity, we will continue celebrating and building our relationships. But death does mean a time of temporary separation and it's not good to die with unfinished business. Dying is an opportunity to deal with the unfinished business in my relationships, so that I can die at peace with God and at peace with the most important people in my life.

FINDING HEALING AND FORGIVENESS

An older woman, whom I shall call Mary, was diagnosed with a very advanced and aggressive form of cancer. She had experienced a life of broken relationships. Her daughter, who was a friend of mine, described her as 'an intensely angry person' with a sharp and destructive tongue. Her daughter had found faith in Christ as a young adult. But Mary had always rejected and rebuffed any attempt to talk about God or the gospel. Then came the sudden and unexpected news that Mary had advanced cancer with only weeks to live. Her daughter told me that as they were sitting in the radiotherapy outpatient department, waiting to be seen, Mary turned to her daughter and said, 'I've just got three questions. One, how can I forgive? Two, how can I be forgiven? And three, what is heaven like?'

Sitting in the noisy outpatient department, her daughter shared the good news of the forgiveness that was to be found in Christ. For the first time, Mary talked about the hidden secret of being abused as a child, and the shame, the hurt, the hatred and the anger which had dominated her life. Mary's daughter gently shared about the forgiveness available in Christ and heaven – a place of safety where nothing could harm her again. From that time in the outpatient department, Mary's life changed. Her daughter told me 'My mother was remade two weeks before she died. I've never seen anything more radical in my life.'

Mary was admitted to a local nursing home. In place of previous bitterness and resentment, there was thankfulness. Her daughter remembers Mary's gratitude on receiving a plate of pureed vegetables. 'I can't believe how kind you are to me,' she said, sitting with her grandchildren. She rejoiced in her new relationship with God: 'You've got no idea what it feels like to pray for the first time.' Her words, once so sharp, were kind and encouraging. 'I feel as though there's an external power to control my tongue,' she shared with her daughter.

Mary died nearly two weeks after that first conversation in the outpatient department, with her daughter holding her hand and singing hymns to her. And as the end came, her daughter whispered to her, 'Your body isn't needed anymore, you're going to receive a brand-new body,' and then very gently, the last breath. Immediately after Mary's death the nurses gathered in her room. 'What an amazing lady. She was so grateful for everything, she was so kind, so gentle, she had no fear about dying. We've never seen anyone die like this.' And her daughter was able to share with them about the Christian faith and the forgiveness and healing that her mother had received. Dying can be an opportunity to find forgiveness and to become what the Bible calls 'a new creation' (2 Cor. 5:17).

BEING THANKFUL

It's an amazing paradox that some of the most thankful people I've met have been those who are dying. Here are the words of a young woman called Ruth van den Brock, who was dying from cystic fibrosis:

> *When it comes to dying well, gratitude has been one of the most transformative things for me, gratitude for my body despite its brokenness, for my medical team despite their limits, for the decay of my lungs because it makes me notice and appreciate most of my waking breaths. A while back, I started praying before I took medications, the way I do before food. 'Lord, thank you for these medications. Thank you, for the people who invented, prescribed and prepared them. Please bless them to my body, and my body in your service.' I began to see them as the blessings they are. Gratitude has changed so much for me, even though I'm still not great at it.*[13]

Isn't it remarkable that as we face the finishing line, we can learn more about gratitude? It's often gratitude for the little things. For that bowl of soup, or watching a bird fly in the sky, or seeing the signs of spring in a garden.

APPROACHING THE FINISHING LINE

My friend Philippa Taylor, who is an elite marathon runner, said that during the race she deliberately thinks about the experience of crossing the finishing line. She imagines the experience in her mind. She tries to anticipate those feelings of achievement, joy, satisfaction and relief that will come as she crosses that line. She visualises sinking her teeth into cake and drinking hot tea and the experience of standing on the podium and receiving the prize.

I had the privilege of supporting another marathon runner friend Alan Toogood, as he was dying from terminal cancer. I had shared with him Philippa's words and he took them to heart. Neither he nor I knew how close he was to the finishing line. His friends had given him a lovely little hand-carved wooden cross, a 'hand-cross' designed to be held in the palm of the hand. This little cross came to hold a great significance for Alan. He took hold of the cross with a resolute grasp and it remained with him throughout his time in hospital. 'I don't normally go in for this kind of thing,' he whispered to me, with a smile. 'But I want to die with this cross in my hand. Mind you, it's an empty cross. It's a reminder of the resurrection.' And only a few hours after our conversation he crossed the finishing line, holding on, like the marathon runner he was, to meet his risen Lord.

Dying well is an opportunity to 'live well right to the end'. But of course dying can also be a time of great testing, a time of trial. It's not possible to go into these topics in detail in this short book. As we approach the end it's important that we have an open and honest conversation with our loved-ones and with the medical professionals who are caring for us. At the back of this book there is a further resources section with helpful suggestions about questions to ask and issues to think about.

FALLING ASLEEP

It is very striking that the New Testament rarely speaks of believers in Christ as 'dying'. Time and again the phrase which is used is that believers 'fall asleep'. Paul uses the phrase repeatedly in his letters and there's no doubt that it was a common expression in the early Christian church. Jesus used the same phrase about the death of Lazarus: 'Our friend Lazarus has fallen asleep; but I am going there to wake him up' (Jn. 11:11).

A sleeping person is in a temporary state of unconsciousness but they are, of course, *still alive*. Throughout the period of sleep, however long it lasts, the person is still there, safe and unharmed. But whilst the period of sleep continues, the person is inaccessible. It's not possible to have a meaningful relationship with a person whilst they are fast asleep! They are alive, but temporarily unreachable.

And we all know that sleep is temporary. From a medical point of view there is a crucial difference between the unconsciousness of natural sleep and the unconsciousness of coma or brain damage. When a person is in a deep coma, it is impossible to know whether they will recover, nor in what state they may recover. It's possible for someone to remain in a coma for weeks or months and then to die without ever regaining consciousness. And if they do awake from coma, they may be totally changed. Their personality may have been irreversibly altered by brain injury. But when a person is sleeping naturally we know that they are going to awake naturally, and when they awake, *they are the same person.* The person is in no way damaged or harmed by the period of sleep.

When Christians die, we fall asleep in Christ. In some mysterious way we remain alive. The risen Lord Jesus himself holds our very being, our personhood, intact and unharmed. Nothing can harm those who have 'fallen asleep in Christ'. So, far from being some kind of gentle euphemism, shielding us from the brutal reality of death, the words 'falling asleep' give deep insight into what it means to die as a Christian believer. From a spiritual point of view Christian believers do not really die. That terrible enemy, death, has in a sense already been absorbed and destroyed by Christ. Jesus has taken the sting, power and grip of death into his own body on the cross and has triumphed over it in his resurrection.

Paul is at pains to encourage the Christians in Thessalonica as they mourn dead loved ones: 'Brothers and sisters, we do not want you to be uninformed about those who sleep in death, so that you do not grieve like the rest of mankind, who have no hope. For we believe that Jesus died and rose again, and so we believe that God will bring with Jesus those who have fallen asleep in him' (1 Thes. 4:13-14). Paul is drawing an explicit distinction between Jesus who *died* and the Christian believers who *fall asleep*. Jesus experienced the full reality of death, so that we might fall asleep in him. And Paul is telling us that we don't need to grieve in the same way as non-Christians do for believers who have died, because we know Jesus is going to wake them up again.

There is also an important psychological truth here. I know that many Christian believers, as they come to the end of their lives, are anxious and fearful about the process of dying. What will it feel like to die? Will I be struggling for breath, experiencing unbearable agony, overwhelmed with fear, sucked into a terrifying black hole of non-existence? It's easy for an over-active imagination to come up with all manner of horrors and nameless fears.

And in response to these fears, our heavenly Father, in his grace and compassion, allows us to practise what it is like to die every single night of our lives. You know precisely what it feels like to die in Christ – it feels like falling asleep. Try to imagine that feeling of being tired, exhausted and drained after a long and gruelling day, and at long last your head touches that soft pillow. All you have to do is to give way to sleep, because you know you are safe, you are secure, you are protected. Falling asleep is not something strange, alien or terrifying. It's an experience that our heavenly Father gives us in advance so that we need not be fearful.

To push the analogy a little further, the person who falls asleep in Christ is not only giving way to sleep after a long, gruelling and exhausting day, they are falling asleep on the first night of the holidays, with all the anticipation, excitement and joy to come when they wake up in the morning. When we fall asleep a final time in this life, as believers in Christ, we will wake up in his presence. With the Apostle Paul, we will be able to say, 'I have fought the good fight, I have finished the race, I have kept the faith' (2 Tim. 4:6-8). The joy of heaven will be ours.

THE EYES OF FAITH

There is an ancient Christian tradition of using the period of preparation for sleep each evening as a way of preparing ourselves for death. This tradition, reaching all the way back to the fourth century, takes Simeon's words in the Gospel of Luke and made them part of the liturgy of evening prayers in services variously called Compline, Vespers or Evensong. Simeon met the newborn baby Jesus in the Temple, and taking the baby into his arms he said those famous words, 'Sovereign Lord, as you have promised, you may now dismiss your servant in peace. For my eyes have seen your salvation, which you have prepared in the sight of all nations' (Lk. 2:25-31).

Simeon had only seen a newborn baby, but with eyes of faith he could see something more. Simeon knew that God's glorious plans and purposes of salvation were underway and they were utterly secure and unbreakable. And with that vision, he could let go. He didn't need to cling on desperately to this life anymore. If we are trusting in Jesus, we too have seen him with the eyes of faith. We too can let go, knowing our forgiveness is guaranteed and our eternity is secure.

As we look back over the long course, the ups and downs of the way that we have come, it's easy to give way to feelings of regret, or maybe to a sense of failure. Maybe there are events earlier on in our race that we bitterly regret, or maybe we feel wounded, angry, resentful or hurt. I close with three short phrases which express the Christian hope and which we need to hang on to as we come to the end of our race:

The good cannot be lost
The evil can be redeemed
And the best is yet to come.

FURTHER RESOURCES

John Wyatt, *Dying Well* (IVP, 2018)

My previous book goes into some of the tests, temptations and challenges that dying can bring, and includes a discussion of helpful questions to ask as death approaches.

Detailed information and documents concerning Advance Care Planning are available at *http://www.goldstandardsframework.org.uk/advance-care-planning*

Detailed information about the UK Mental Capacity Act 2005 is available at *http://www.legislation.gov.uk/ukpga/2005/9/contents*

More information is also found at *https://www.gov.uk/government/publications/mental-capacity-act-code-of-practice*

Information and guidance about Lasting Power of Attorney is available from the UK government website at *https://www.gov.uk/power-of-attorney/overview*

Information and guidance about Advance Decisions to Refuse Treatment is available from the NHS website at *https://www.nhs.uk/conditions/end-of-life-care/advance-decision-to-refuse-treatment/*

ENDNOTES

1 UK Office Of National Statistics: https://www.ons.gov.uk/peoplepopulationandcommunity/birthsdeathsandmarriages/lifeexpectancies/bulletins/pastandprojecteddatafromtheperiodandcohortlifetables/2020baseduk1981to2070 [accessed 18/11/22].

2 Valentina Romei, 'Europe's Demographic Time Bomb', Financial Times, 13 January 2020 [accessed 7/12/22].

3 Ian Knox, *Finishing Well: A God's-eye View of Ageing* (SPCK, 2020), p. 18.

4 Frederick Buechner, 'Vocation' Frederick Buechner.com, 18 July 2021 https://www.frederickbuechner.com/quote-of-the-day/2021/7/18/vocation [accessed 25/11/22].

5 Ian Knox, *Finishing Well: A God's-eye View of Ageing* (SPCK, 2020), p. 162.

6 The phrase 'mutual burdensomeness' is from Gilbert Meilaender, *Bioethics: A Primer for Christians* (4th edition), (WB Eerdmans, 2020), p. 3.

7 Gilbert Meilaender 'I Want to Burden My Loved Ones' First Things, March 2010, https://www.firstthings.com/article/2010/03/i-want-to-burden-my-loved-ones [accessed 18/11/22].

8 The story of the little girl who is afraid of the dark is taken from John Wyatt, *Matters of Life and Death* (2nd edition), (IVP, 2009).

9 John Dunlop, *Finishing Well to the Glory of God: Strategies from a Christian Physician* (Crossway, 2011), p. 53.

10 Ibid. p. 40.

11 C.S. Lewis, *A Severe Mercy* (Hodder & Stoughton, 2011).

12 Ibid. p. 12.

13 Quoted in John Wyatt, *Dying Well* (IVP, 2018), p. 24.